The Teen Who Invented Television

Philo T. Farnsworth and His Awesome Invention

Edwin Brit Wyckoff

Enslow Elementary

an imprint of

Enslow Publishers, Inc.

40 Industrial Road
Box 398
Berkeley Heights, NJ 07922
USA

http://www.enslow.com

Content Advisers
Kent M. Farnsworth
Son of Philo T. Farnsworth
Steward, Farnsworth Archives:
  http://www.philotfarnsworth.com

Evan I. Schwartz
Author, *The Last Lone Inventor:*
  A Tale of Genius, Deceit
  & the Birth of Television

Series Literacy Consultant
Allan A. De Fina, Ph.D.
Past President of the New Jersey Reading Association
Professor, Department of Literacy Education
New Jersey City University

Acknowledgment

The publisher thanks Kent M. Farnsworth for providing many insights and photos for the publication of this book.

Enslow Elementary, an imprint of Enslow Publishers, Inc.

Enslow Elementary® is a registered trademark of Enslow Publishers, Inc.

Library of Congress Cataloging-in-Publication Data

Wyckoff, Edwin Brit.
   The teen who invented television : Philo T. Farnsworth and his awesome invention/Edwin Brit Wyckoff.
      p. cm. — (Genius at work! Great inventor biographies)
   Includes bibliographical references and index.
   ISBN-13: 978-0-7660-2845-6
   ISBN-10: 0-7660-2845-3
      1. Farnsworth, Philo Taylor, 1906–1971—Juvenile literature. 2. Electric engineers—United States—Biography—Juvenile literature. 3. Inventors—United States—Biography—Juvenile literature.
   4. Television—History—Juvenile literature. I. Title.
   TK6635.F3W93 2007
   621.3092—dc22
                              2006034683

Printed in the United States of America

10 9 8 7 6 5 4 3 2 1

To Our Readers
We have done our best to make sure all Internet addresses in this book were active and appropriate when we went to press. However, the author and the publisher have no control over and assume no liability for the material available on those Internet sites or on other Web sites they may link to. Any comments or suggestions can be sent by e-mail to comments@enslow.com or to the address on the back cover.

Every effort has been made to locate all copyright holders of material used in this book. If any errors or omissions have occurred, corrections will be made in future editions of this book.

Photo Credits: Alvis E. Hendley, p. 20; Courtesy MagazineArt.org, p. 8 (both); Culver Pictures, p. 10; David Sarnoff Library, p. 25; Farnsworth Archives, pp. 3 (background), 4, 6, 7, 13, 15, 17, 21, 22, 23, 26, 27 (both); © iStockphoto.com/ Grafissimo, p. 3 (top inset); Courtesy Lee Schaeffer, p. 11; Manuscripts Division, University of Utah Libraries, pp. 1 (left), 16, 18, 24, 28 (inset); NASA/Scan by Kipp Teague, p. 28; Utah State Historical Society, all rights reserved (photograph has been color-enhanced), pp. 1 (right), 3 (bottom inset); Wisconsin Historical Society, p. 12.

Front Cover Photos: © 2007 JupiterImages Corporation (background); Utah State Historical Society, all rights reserved (inset, photograph has been color-enhanced).

Back Cover Photo: © 2007 JupiterImages Corporation.

Contents

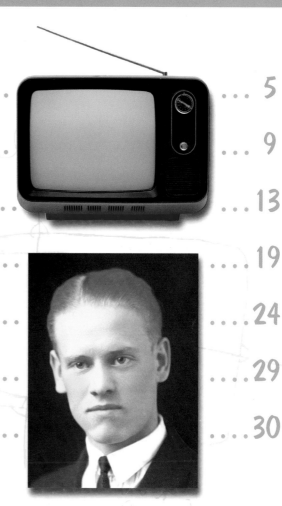

Philo T. Farnsworth, 1936

Chapter 1

Dangerous Dreams

Three powerful horses were plowing the potato fields back and forth, slowly and steadily. Fourteen-year-old Philo Farnsworth held the reins loosely. He seemed to be slipping into sleep as some of the reins fell from his hands. His father could see a terrible accident about to happen. Shouting would have scared the horses. So without a word, he raced across the field and scooped up the fallen reins. The horses stopped. Philo snapped wide awake. His father was very angry. But Philo's eyes were filled with excitement.

He had just dreamed up how to build a magnetic lock for an automobile. That idea won him twenty-five dollars in a contest run by a scientific magazine. Twenty-five dollars was a lot of money in 1920, when an ice cream cone cost only a nickel.

Philo Taylor Farnsworth was born on August 19, 1906, in Beaver, Utah. He had two younger brothers and two younger sisters. His parents, Lewis and Serena, were farmers. They were always looking for cheaper, better land on which to raise their crops. In 1918, when Philo was about twelve, the family packed up and moved from Utah to Rigby, Idaho. Young Philo drove the horses that pulled one of their covered wagons. He was thinking about new inventions all the way.

The family's new farm was wonderful. Unlike most farms at that time, it had electric lights.

This is Philo's father, Lewis Farnsworth. The two of them were very close.

Exploring the new farm was fun. The children found a pile of old, broken motors to play with.

For Philo, the biggest treasure was up in the attic. There he found lots of science magazines with names like *Modern Electrics, Electrical Experimenter*, and *Radio News*. He read them over and over. He learned how airplanes lifted off the ground and how radios were built.

Philo was born in this cabin in Beaver, Utah. At the time the town was called Indian Creek.

He read about ideas for the future, like spaceships and collecting energy from the sun. He thought he could someday invent things, too—but first he had to learn everything he could about science.

One day, the lights went out on the farm. The electric generator had stopped working.

Philo liked to read these magazines.
They told of ideas about life in the future.

Repairmen were called to fix it. After they left, the lights went out again. Philo thought he had seen the men make a mistake. The whole family watched as Philo fixed the mistake in minutes. The lights came on again.

Chapter 2

Flying Pictures

Radios were new in the early 1900s. People would sit and watch them, even though radios just played music, news, and talk shows. There was really nothing to see.

Philo's scientific magazines began reporting about something called television. They said it would make pictures "fly" through the air like radio. But television was an idea that still had to be figured out.

Philo was captivated. He dreamed that he would make a fortune by bringing pictures into every home. But he was sure that the television systems described in his magazines would not work very well. He knew that he could do better.

Philo did not want to use moving parts, such as spinning wheels, the way other inventors

People liked to sit around watching the radio together as they listened to programs like *The Eveready Hour.*

wanted to. They were not fast enough to make a clear picture. He believed in using electrons. Electrons are tiny parts of everything in the world. Philo wanted to learn how to use them to make electronic television pictures.

It was the summer of 1921, and Philo was just fifteen years old. He searched for one big idea

Philo's magazines described television systems that were mechanical. This television receiver, made by John Logie Baird, used a spinning wheel inside.

that would allow him to use electrons. Hour after hour, he held the leather reins as the farm horses slowly worked the fields. Squinting in the sun, he would watch row after row of earth line up. One day, all of a sudden, he had an exciting idea. He imagined row after row of electrons lining up

Philo was riding a disk harrow like this one when he had his idea. When the disks were dragged through the dirt, many even rows were created. This way a farmer could quickly prepare a field for planting seeds.

to make pictures. As the electrons moved, the pictures moved, almost like crops blowing in the wind.

In his mind, Philo imagined a camera shaped like a glass bottle. Light from the object being photographed would travel into the bottle through the flat end. Then the light would be changed into rows of electrons inside the bottle. Another bottle could be the television screen. Rows of electrons inside this second bottle would become a picture flashed onto its flat end. Philo could almost shout with happiness. He was going to invent television.

Chapter 3

The Amazing Student

In September of 1921, Philo entered Rigby High School. First-year science classes were too easy for him. He wanted to skip to senior science classes. The teacher, Justin Tolman, first said no. Philo asked him every

Rigby High School in Rigby, Idaho, was where Philo became friends with his science teacher, Justin Tolman.

day. Finally, Mr. Tolman let him sit in the back of the room during the class.

After school one day, Mr. Tolman found Philo filling every inch of the blackboard with drawings. Philo started talking faster and faster—about television. He took a page from his teacher's notebook to make more drawings. Someday that page of scribbles would be very, very important. Mr. Tolman told Philo to keep quiet about television so no one else could steal his ideas.

Although he was always busy thinking, Philo still found time for fun. He learned how to play the violin and joined a band. This serious young man was a great dancer and a good actor. He also became a very good tennis player.

In the cold, hard winter of 1924, Philo's father returned from a long trip and became very sick. He died when Philo was only seventeen. Philo had to work to support the family. He earned a high school diploma and had a real love for learning. But he had no way to pay for college.

Still, Philo enrolled at Brigham Young University in Salt Lake City, Utah. He worked as a school janitor to pay for his classes. He still

This is the sketch of a television camera that Philo drew for Mr. Tolman. Light from a picture hits the camera on the left, labeled "optical image." Electrons scan the optical image and change it into an electronic signal on the right, labeled "electron image."

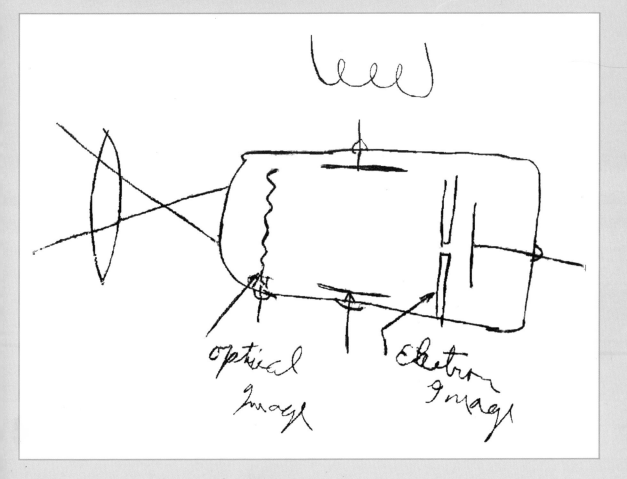

Philo (center) acted in the play *Charm School* at Brigham Young University.

loved music and dancing and parties. He also started dating Elma Gardner, his neighbor. Everyone called her Pem. Philo was so quiet that Pem was not sure he cared about her.

Philo took the test to become an officer in the navy. His score was second highest in the whole country. He was

Elma "Pem" Gardner

accepted by the United States Naval Academy in Annapolis, Maryland. But once he was there, he learned that the government would own any inventions he thought up while he was in the navy. He asked his mother to tell the school she needed him at home, and he was allowed to leave.

Les Gorrell (left), Philo (center), and George Everson worked together to start creating electronic television.

Chapter 4

Meeting the Money Men

Philo went back to college for another year, but money problems forced him to drop out. He took a full-time job working for two smart young men. George Everson and Leslie Gorrell were in the business of raising money for charities that helped needy people in Salt Lake City. Working late one night, he started telling them his ideas. He talked faster and faster—about television.

Everson suddenly asked, "How much? How much to make a working model?" That was a scary question. Philo answered, "Five thousand dollars." Everson offered, "We'll invest six thousand. And the workshop has to be in California."

Philo was only nineteen, and he was starting a new life. He telephoned Pem. "Can you be ready to get married in three days?" So Philo and Pem married on May 27, 1926. They took a train to Los Angeles, California, just one day after their wedding.

Their apartment was very small. The dining room table was covered with Philo's inventions.

In this laboratory at 202 Green Street, San Francisco, Philo built the first electronic television system.

Closets were jammed with his tools. Pem learned how to weld metal together and how to make technical drawings. George Everson took charge of cooking. All of them would eat and work together six nights a week.

Their $6,000 did not last long. Everson and Gorrell went looking for investors, or people to give them money. They found a rich banker, James Fagan. He growled, "This television is a . . . fool idea. But somebody ought to put money into it." He gave them $25,000.

Cliff Gardner, Pem's brother, found a new way to make the glass "bottles" Philo needed for his television system.

The team moved to San Francisco, California. Philo bought new tools and hired Cliff Gardner, Pem's brother. Cliff quickly learned how to blow fiery hot glass into tubes with a special flat end. Some of the tubes became the camera, which Philo called an image dissector. Others were turned into receivers, or screens, which would show the

21

pictures made by lines of electrons. The image dissector and the receiver were the "bottles" that Philo had seen in his mind in 1921 on his family's farm.

It was time to tell the whole world Philo's secret ideas. On January 7, 1927, Philo asked the government for patents to protect his camera and receiver ideas from being stolen by other inventors. He tested his system in his laboratory in San Francisco in September of that year. He turned on the power. He flipped all the switches. Everyone waited and worried. Slowly, an image of a line formed on the receiver. "There you are," Philo said, "electronic television."

Philo holds an image dissector. In front of him is an early television camera.

This early television picture of Pem from 1930 shows the lines of the electrons.

In 1928, a newspaper in San Francisco ran an article about Philo, with a huge headline:

MAN'S INVENTION TO REVOLUTIONIZE TELEVISION. FARNSWORTH'S SYSTEM EMPLOYS NO MOVING PARTS.

In August 1930, Philo was given two patents for his television camera and receiver. He was only twenty-four years old.

The Patent War

A very important businessman visited Philo's laboratory to see the system work. David Sarnoff

screen

This is a Farnsworth Television Receiver from 1930.

was the president of the giant Radio Corporation of America, or RCA. He looked at everything very carefully. He said, "There is nothing we need here." Then he shocked everybody. Sarnoff offered $100,000 to buy the whole laboratory. He wanted Philo to go to work for RCA. Philo's answer was a flat, final no.

Sarnoff did not like being told no by anybody. And he

wanted Philo's inventions. He would fight to get them. His company had lots of lawyers. They attacked Philo in court, saying that he was not really the inventor of electronic television.

David Sarnoff knew that Philo's television patents were worth millions of dollars.

How could Philo prove that he had his ideas for television before anyone else? He thought and thought. Then he came up with the answer—he had told Justin Tolman.

Philo's lawyers went looking for his old science teacher. Mr. Tolman went down to his basement. When he climbed back up the stairs, he was waving a page from his old notebook. It was covered with Philo's drawing from way back in 1922, when he was just a teenager.

The United States Patent Office approved Philo's television ideas and drawings with a patent.

A patent says powerful things:

1. The ideas are workable.
2. The ideas are new—no one else has yet presented them.
3. If people want to use the ideas, they have to pay money, called a royalty, to the owner of the patent.

Justin Tolman, here with Philo, helped him to win the court case against David Sarnoff and RCA.

Tough, powerful David Sarnoff and his lawyers lost the court case in 1935. Philo was exhausted.

Sarnoff may have lost the fight, but he was a good businessman. In October of 1939, he offered to pay one million dollars over ten years to use Philo's patents and pay a royalty every time he used the invention. Sarnoff hated paying royalties. But he had to pay Philo.

The farm boy who invented electronic television when he was only fifteen years old never stopped dreaming up and inventing new things. He received more than one hundred patents for new and better radios, television systems, and military tools. On July 20, 1969, he watched American astronauts walking on the moon. The astronauts sent back sharp, clear pictures. The pictures traveled 238,900 miles from the moon using a very small version of Philo's image dissector.

Philo T. Farnsworth died in Salt Lake City on March 11, 1971. He was sixty-four years old. In 1984, he was elected to the National Inventors Hall of Fame by

screen

Philo adjusts the dials as he looks into an early television receiver. The round object at the top right is the speaker.

Philo would go on to own a television recording studio. Here he stands with the first mobile television camera.

Once Philo saw astronauts walking on the moon on television, he knew his invention had been worth all the work.

the U.S. Patent Office. The young farm boy from Utah had spent his whole life studying, thinking, and dreaming science. Philo Farnsworth always believed he could be a great inventor, and he succeeded.

1906 Born on August 19 in Beaver, Utah.

1922 Shows television drawings to his science teacher, Justin Tolman.

1924 Father dies; Philo attends Brigham Young University for two years.

1926 Creates partnership with George Everson and Leslie Gorrell to develop television; marries Elma "Pem" Gardner and moves to California.

1927 Files patents for television system; tests system successfully in San Francisco.

1930 Is granted patents for television camera and receiver.

1934 Radio Corporation of America loses court case against Philo.

1939 RCA pays one million dollars to license Philo's television patents.

1971 Dies on March 11 in Salt Lake City, Utah; is buried in Provo, Utah.

1984 Is elected to National Inventors Hall of Fame by United States Patent Office.

disk harrow—A farming tool that creates many even rows of earth for planting crops.

electric—Using energy made from moving electrons, usually through wires.

electron—A tiny electrical part of every material thing in the world.

electronic—Using electrons.

generator—A machine that changes power from a source like gasoline into electricity.

investor—Someone who supplies money for an idea and expects to earn more money in return.

laboratory—A workshop for scientific experiments and tests.

mechanical—Using moving parts.

weld—To press and melt two pieces of metal together by running electricity through them.

working model—An early example of an invention that works. It may be very small or without all the details of the final piece.

Books

McPherson, Stephanie Sammartino. *TV's Forgotten Hero: The Story of Philo Farnsworth*. Minneapolis: Carolrhoda Books, 1996.

Roberts, Russell. *Philo Farnsworth Invents TV*. Hockessin, Del.: Mitchell Lane Publishers, 2005.

Stille, Darlene R. *Television*. Minneapolis: Compass Point Books, 2002.

Internet Addresses

Biography of Phil Farnsworth from By Kids for Kids
http://www.bkfk.com/inventors/farnsworth-filo.asp

History of Television
http://history.sandiego.edu/gen/recording/television1.html

Index